Virginia Hall

Most Dangerous

Women of War #4:

History Nerds

While every precaution has been taken in the preparation of this book, the publisher assumes no responsibility for errors or omissions, or for damages resulting from the use of the information contained herein.
Virginia Hall
Women of War - Book 4
Copyright © 2023 History Nerds.
ISBN: 9798223468912
Written by History Nerds.

Introduction

Virginia Hall, an extraordinary figure whose life's journey weaves a tapestry of bravery, tenacity, and unwavering commitment to a higher cause, is a historic figure whose actions never cease to inspire. In the following pages, we embark on a voyage through the tumultuous chapters of the 20th century, guided by the unparalleled story of a woman whose impact reverberated far beyond her era.

Born into a world marked by upheaval and transformation when wars reigned, Virginia Hall emerged as a symbol of unwavering determination against the backdrop of two World Wars and the intricate web of espionage that defined an era. A daughter of privilege and refinement, her path took an unexpected turn when adversity struck, altering the course of her life in ways unforeseen. As we delve into the depths of her experiences, we will witness the evolution of a young woman who faced setbacks that would have defeated most, instead harnessing her adversity to catalyze her unyielding spirit.

This biography is a testament to Virginia Hall's extraordinary accomplishments as a trailblazer, a spy, and a changemaker. Her relentless pursuit of justice, equality, and freedom intertwined with her pivotal role in covert operations during World War II, serving as a linchpin in the fight against tyranny. From the clandestine corridors of espionage to the secret passages of power, her story unravels the intricacies of her intelligence work, offering a rare glimpse into the world of espionage and the courage it demanded.

Beyond her exploits in espionage, Virginia Hall's legacy resonates as a symbol of the things a woman can achieve once she endeavors to do so. She carved a path for herself and women everywhere in a world resistant to change, defying convention and shattering glass ceilings.

Her journey invites us to reflect on the transformative power of resilience and the capacity of an individual to shape the course of history, regardless of the challenges encountered. As we embark on this literary journey through the life of Virginia Hall, let us be inspired by her audacious spirit, strategic brilliance, and unwavering commitment to the causes she held dear.

Her story is not just a recounting of the past but a beacon of courage that illuminates our present and future. Through meticulous research, personal accounts, and historical context, this biography seeks to honor Virginia Hall's enduring legacy while weaving a narrative that captures the essence of a woman who dared to defy limitations and, in doing so, altered the trajectory of history. Her life reminds us that even in the face of adversity, ordinary individuals can achieve extraordinary feats that shape the world in ways unimaginable.

Chapter I

Virginia Hall was a remarkable figure in World War II history, known for her extraordinary contributions as a spy and for overcoming various challenges throughout her life. Born on April 6, 1906, in Baltimore, Maryland, she became one of the most successful and celebrated agents of the Special Operations Executive (SOE) and the Office of Strategic Services (OSS) during World War II. Virginia Hall was born into a prominent family with a strong military tradition. Her father, Edwin Lee Hall, was a successful businessman, and her mother, Barbara Virginia Hammel, hailed from a well-respected Baltimore family. Early in her life, her parents provided her with a good education for the time. She attended Roland Park Country School, Radcliffe College of Harvard, and Barnard College of Columbia. She studied French, Italian, and German there, which was an enormous privilege. Her studies gave her skills that would be immensely useful later in life. Subsequently, Virginia attended George

Washington University, furthering her study of French and Economics.

Virginia Hall was a highly educated woman and very accomplished, according to the standards of the time. She also traveled the world, a thing not all women of the time could boast of. Virginia was keen to finish her studies in Europe, so she traveled there, studying for a time in Austria, France, and Germany. All this experience, of course, opened new horizons and opportunities for her. Thanks to this, she managed to land an appointment as a Consular Service clerk at the United States Embassy in Warsaw, Poland. She began working there in 1931.

So, as we see, Virginia Hall had a remarkable childhood and youth. This colorful childhood would prepare her well for a future life in espionage. The Hall family was very successful in Baltimore and thus paved the way for Virginia's successes. Edwin was a successful entrepreneur, and his wife Barbara was a strong and accomplished woman. Their children, Virginia and John, naturally followed in their parents' footsteps. The Hall family enjoyed outdoor adventures on their large family farm and overseas travels. They'd often travel to Europe for holidays, and that love of travel would remain with Virginia in adulthood. It also gave her an adventurous and outgoing character. As a student, she was very bright and became the class president of Roland Park Country School. She was the editor-in-chief of the school newspaper and even the field hockey team captain. She shied away from nothing and built her character well.

In time, Virginia grew up into a natural leader, a strong and independent woman with a lot of self-confidence. The yearbook, which survived from that time, says of Virginia Hall as the *"most original of our class, comfortable in any situation - nothing daunted her."* She was a woman shaped for great deeds. Finding work as a clerk in the American Embassy in Warsaw was an outstanding achievement for an educated and

adventurous woman such as herself. It was a
lofty position at the time, and it paid well. In time,
she served in several European posts, including
in Turkey. She was transferred there in the early
1930s, specifically to Smyrna, now known as
Izmir. Working in Turkey was fine, but Virginia
was restless, always ambitious and wanting more.
She desired to join the Diplomatic Corps, with
few women employed then. Before any of that
could be achieved, however, disaster struck.

In 1933, Virginia was on a hunting trip in Turkey.
On the shores of the Gediz Peninsula, she was
hunting Gallinago, better known as Snipes, which
are small wading marsh birds. While carrying her
shotgun, she tripped on a wire and sustained a
self-inflicted gunshot wound in her lower leg.
Gangrene quickly set in, bringing Virginia to the
brink of death. The injury was awful because the
gun was so close to her foot when it fired. The
shotgun pellets all but destroyed her foot. Soft
tissue and bone damage were immense, and what
is more, the wound was severely contaminated.

Parts of her boot were embedded in it, as were the grass and pieces of cloth. By the time she was brought to the hospital in the local town of Smyrna, well over an hour had passed, allowing infection and gangrene to appear. Hearing of her case, Dr. Lorrin Shepard, head of the Istanbul American Hospital, rushed to Smyrna to help. He quickly determined that amputating below the knee was the only effective way to save Virginia's life, but the patient was unconscious, and Dr. Shepard could not discuss it with her. He was unwilling to risk her life by waiting for her to wake up, so Dr. Shepard moved forward with the amputation, amputating her left leg below the knee. The procedure saved her life.

After the operation, she was given leave from the State Department and journeyed back to the family farm in Parkton, Maryland, where she recovered and learned to walk with a prosthetic limb. Virginia maintained a positive attitude and would not be stopped by her disability. She named her fake leg "Cuthbert". Slowly, she learned to walk with it. It was not a modern, inconspicuous prosthetic limb like the ones we have today. It was more clunky, made from painted wood that often didn't fit too well, and created sores and discomfort. "Cuthbert" was attached to Virginia via leather belts and had an aluminum foot. It weighed around 7 pounds, which made walking even more difficult. As a result, Virginia had a noticeable limp. M.R.D. Foot, a British political and military historian and former British Army intelligence officer with the SOE during World War II, is quoted as saying:

"She was a journalist from Baltimore, conspicuous by reddish hair, a strong American accent, an artificial foot, and an imperturbable temper; she took risks often but intelligently."

Virginia's disability would not stop her nor diminish her adventurous spirit. After a brief and successful recovery, Virginia returned to work as a consular clerk in Venice, Italy and Tallinn, Estonia. These two assignments were another addition to her already overflowing resume. She was well-traveled, with plenty of experience, knowledge, and fluency in different languages, and in the late 1930s, when the world stood on the brink of another global war, such skills were essential.

In 1937, Virginia decided to pursue her dream of joining the Diplomatic Corps, but the rules for entering it were stringent. The State Department prohibited employees with physical disabilities from joining the Diplomatic Corps. Virginia, now an amputee, was barred from testing. If she had not been a person with a disability, these skills would have quickly gained her entry into the Department of State and the diplomatic positions she desired, but alas, rules were rules. Virginia was furious and wrote a heated appeal to the Secretary of State, Cordell Hull. Hull dismissed the letter and stated that Virginia *"should be satisfied"* with her existing career prospects. He wrote that she *"could become a fine career girl in the Consular Service."* There was no further possibility for appeal. Hall's hopes had been crushed by the unfortunate accident she suffered and the strictness of the Department's rules. Eventually, Virginia resigned in 1939 while still a consular clerk.

Having newly resigned, Virginia had a desire to seek adventure once again. To explore Europe in a way that she always wanted and should have. She traveled to it but never for pleasure - always for business. Now was the time, but it was not the *right* time. In a destined turn of events, Virginia traveled to Paris, France, on the eve of World War II. She went there to find a new meaning in life and experience the French capital's thrill and adventure. Instead, Virginia discovered war and ruin. She found adventure of a different, darker type. So, in February 1940, early in the war, Virginia became an ambulance driver for the French Ambulance Service. There, she witnessed the horrors of war first-hand. The German invasion of France was swift and brutal.

Chapter II

Known as the Battle of France or the Fall of France, this was a pivotal and rapid military campaign during World War II. It marked the defeat of France and its allies, including the United Kingdom, at the hands of the German forces led by Adolf Hitler. The invasion had far-reaching consequences for the course of the war and the shaping of Europe. The German offensive began on May 10, 1940, with a massive and unexpected attack through Belgium, Luxembourg, and the Netherlands. This maneuver was designed to bypass the heavily fortified Maginot Line, a series of defenses built by the French along their border with Germany. German forces swiftly advanced, using innovative tactics and combining armored units with infantry. The German forces managed to outflank and encircle a significant portion of the French and British troops, pushing them back toward the English Channel. The trapped Allied forces were moved into a pocket around Dunkirk, where a desperate evacuation operation, aptly named the Dunkirk evacuation, occurred between May 26 and June 4. Though chaotic, this evacuation saved many British and French soldiers. Paris fell to Germany on June 14, 1940, as the German forces continued their advance. The French government surrendered, and the Germans occupied the city. This event marked a significant, symbolic and strategic victory for Adolf Hitler and his people. On June 22, 1940, France signed an armistice with Germany, effectively ending the active phase of hostilities on the Western Front. The armistice divided France into occupied and unoccupied zones, with the northern and western parts under German control and the southern part governed by the collaborationist Vichy government.

One of the critical factors that contributed to such a swift and brutal German victory in France was the "blitzkrieg." Blitzkrieg, often translated as "lightning war," was a military tactic used by the German military during World War II. It emphasized the use of speed, surprise, and coordinated movements of mechanized forces, infantry, and air support to achieve swift and overwhelming victories on the battlefield. Blitzkrieg tactics were instrumental in the early successes of the German military in campaigns such as the invasions of Poland, France, and other European countries.

Blitzkrieg relied on effectively coordinating different military branches, particularly armored units (tanks), infantry, and air support. These forces would work together in a synchronized manner to exploit weaknesses in the enemy's defenses. These Blitzkrieg tactics aimed to catch the enemy off guard by launching unexpected and rapid attacks. Deceptive movements, diversionary attacks, and misleading intelligence were often used to confuse and disorient the enemy. One of the central tenets of Blitzkrieg was the rapid movement of mechanized forces, often using tanks and armored vehicles, to break through enemy lines. These fast-moving units would exploit openings and push deep into enemy territory. All this worked brilliantly in France; the country was overrun, and its dated mechanization was quickly devastated by the modern German armor and firepower.

Virginia Hall had first-hand experience of the quick and violent conflict that erupted in France. As the National Socialists entered a conquered Paris, Virginia's short but courageous career as a French ambulance driver ended. It did not mean there was no work for Virginia Hall because work would soon reach her doorstep. Even though war had swept the globe, she was well aware that the world was about to change, and she wanted to be a part of that change and was willing to act. Realizing that the war was lost, Virginia Hall fled Paris. Soon after the fall of France, Virginia found herself in Spain. There, by pure chance, she met George Bellows, a British intelligence officer. Their meeting would be the chance of a lifetime, an occurrence that was nothing short of *fate*. George Bellows had a job opportunity for someone like Virginia, extraordinary work.

As Virginia and George got to know each other, George was incredibly impressed with Virginia's character and energy. He knew that she was the type of person he was looking for. Still not revealing too much, George Bellows offered her a job and provided the telephone number of a "friend" working in England, where he could find employment for her. Virginia was eager to find out more and jumped at the chance. The person she was to meet was none other than Nicolas Bodington, a key figure in the newly created Special Operations Executive (SEO), also known as "The Baker Street Irregulars." British Prime Minister Winston Churchill established the Special Operation Executive. His idea was to support the various resistance movements within Europe and promote sabotage operations amongst them. In that way, he would further contribute to a speedy defeat of the enemy. Alas, for all its ideas, the newly established SOE had a poor grasp of the European theater. It was said that Michelin guides had to be used to understand France's layout better.

Virginia Hall was the ideal woman for the newly formed SOE. What prevented her from working for the American Diplomatic Corps became an asset with the SOE. She was a candidate they desperately needed. She was confident and outgoing, experienced and liberal, intelligent and well-traveled. Her life shaped her to be the ideal secret agent, and the leaders of the SOE quickly recognized that. So it was that after her initial meeting, Virginia was formally recruited into SOE in 1941. She underwent training and was given her first instructions.

So it was that the pathways of life led Virginia to a wholly new chapter, one that she didn't even dream about. With the war erupting all across Europe, she found herself with a new mission, a goal to help others and make a difference where it mattered. During the entire war, SOE would send a total of 41 female agents to France. Only 26 would survive to the end of the war, which tells us how dangerous and lethal this work could be. Her work was not easy and could quickly end in disaster.

Virginia's career began in "Vichy France." On August 23, 1941, she arrived in the French town of Vichy, being chosen as SOE's first female resident agent. She used a false name, forged papers, and worked undercover as a reporter for the New York Post. Her headquarters were established in the Haute Loire department, more precisely between Lyon and Toulouse. Her mission, of utmost importance for the SOE, was code-named Geologist 5 and aimed to provide SOE with information about Vichy France. This information included reports on all new political developments, economic conditions, and the attitude of the locals - how willing they were to resist the Germans.

"Vichy France" is not only a town but also refers to the collaborationist French government that existed during World War II under the leadership of Marshal Philippe Pétain. It takes its name from the town of Vichy, where the government was based. The Vichy regime emerged in 1940 following the German invasion of France and the subsequent armistice signed between Nazi Germany and France. Operating from Vichy, the government cooperated closely with Nazi Germany in various areas, including security and economy. It enacted anti-Semitic policies that discriminated against Jews and supported the deportation of many to concentration camps. Despite this collaboration, segments of the French population engaged in resistance against both the occupiers and the Vichy government. The regime's legitimacy waned as Allied forces liberated France in 1944, leading to its dissolution and the arrest of Pétain. Vichy France remains a subject of historical debate and sensitivity in France, representing the complex moral and political challenges faced during the occupation.

Having the cover of a New York Post reporter,

Virginia Hall could freely interview people, which proved a valuable asset in her undercover work. She would also gather information and file stories with details useful to British military planners. In no time, Virginia proved to be an ideal secret agent.

"Virginia Hall left no memoir, granted no interviews, and spoke little about her overseas life--even with relatives. She...received our country's Distinguished Service Cross, the only civilian woman in the Second World War to do so. But she refused all but a private ceremony with OSS chief Donovan--even a presentation by President Truman." - Craig R. Gralley

During World War II, agents played a crucial role in intelligence gathering, sabotage, and covert operations on behalf of various nations. These agents operated behind enemy lines, often at significant personal risk, to gather information, disrupt enemy activities, and support resistance movements. Usually, they were tasked with gathering valuable information about enemy troop movements, military installations, industrial production, and other strategic matters. They often operated in disguise and used various techniques to blend in with local populations and gather information discreetly.

Engaging in sabotage operations, such as destroying infrastructure, disrupting supply lines, and damaging vital installations, these activities aimed to hinder the enemy's war effort and create confusion. They used encoded messages to communicate with their handlers and headquarters. Codebreaking played a significant role in deciphering enemy messages, allowing agents to securely transmit and receive critical information. Before embarking to Europe, SOE agents were trained in various skills, including weapons handling, radio operation, and survival techniques. They were often tasked with infiltrating enemy lines to gather information or carry out operations. Infiltration required careful planning, disguises, and cover stories. Exfiltration involves safely extracting covert operatives from dangerous situations.

The SOE's work didn't stop there. Sometimes, being a secret agent was not enough. Some agents operated as double agents, feeding misinformation to the enemy to deceive and confuse their intelligence efforts. This tactic misled the enemy about the Allies' true intentions. Being a double agent was arduous work, as one was constantly under suspicion, usually watched closely and followed. Spies faced significant risks, including capture, torture, and execution if their true identities were discovered. Many agents displayed tremendous bravery and dedication to their missions, even in grave danger. Ultimately, the hard work of these personnel played a critical role in shaping the outcomes of battles, campaigns, and even the war itself by providing vital intelligence to military commanders and decision-makers.

"Spy agencies were expanding to cope with the need for covert action in countries where insurrection had to be plotted under the noses of occupying Germans. The French Resistance called on women's courage, as did the Special Operations Executive, or SOE, created by Winston Churchill to "set Europe ablaze" by planting bombs, stealing plans, and stoking internal opposition. Colloquially known as the Ministry of Ungentlemanly Warfare, the SOE sought agents willing to parachute into occupied France or be off-loaded by air or sea. Behind enemy lines, SOE operatives had to recruit locals as agents, establish networks, receive clandestine shipments, set up safe houses, manage communications, suss out traitors."

-   Liza Mundy, in her article "Female Spies and Their Secrets"

published in <u>The Atlantic</u>

Chapter III

Virginia Hall was quick to establish herself as a
spy. One could even call her a "pioneer" in the
newly created world of female agents during
World War II. A "secret agent handbook" did not
exist for her to learn from. This meant that she
was the one to create the rules, a spy "guidebook"
of her own. The SOE historian M.R.D. Foot said
that Hall had the difficult job of teaching herself
the *"exacting tasks of being available, arranging
contacts, recommending who to bribe and where to
hide, soothing the jagged nerves of agents on the run
and supervising the distribution of wireless sets."*
Virginia made her base of operations in the city of
Lyon, France. Paris was under German
occupation and thus a dangerous place to work.
To fit into the social network of Lyon and remain
inconspicuous, Virginia had to abandon her chic
and modern fashion style that was so popular in
Paris. Instead, she would dress plainly and
quickly change between outfits to fit different

roles and adapt to different situations. This was a common tactic of spies and agents.

As one of the leading agents, Virginia created and expanded her spy network, code-named Heckler. This network was one of the most important logistical hubs in war-torn France. Virginia even went beyond her usual duties and recruited new spies. One of these was the agent Suzanne Berillon, a former government censor whom Virginia often called "my unofficial Vichy correspondent." She established a chain of 90 operatives in South France. With Virginia's help, this group of agents provided intelligence on fuel and ammunition depots, troop movements of the German army, the enemy's industrial production and capacities, and the location of German submarine bases that were under construction at the time. The latter was successfully bombed by Allied airplanes thanks to the work of the agents. Of course, such valuable information could not be sent directly for fear of discovery. Messages often had to be sent from one point to another. Virginia often sent her encoded messages via Western Union telegrams to her "middle-man" George Backer at the New York Post, who would then forward the message to SOE in London.

In no time, the British were enhancing their agent operations, recruiting more and more capable men and women and parachuting them into France, establishing many networks across the country. Still, Heckler was first on the ground and was centrally situated. Through her early work in the group, Virginia Hall became an expert at support operation - she organized local resistance movement groups, supplied other operatives with money, supplies, and weapons, helped downed airmen to escape or find refuge, offered safe houses and medical assistance to wounded pilots and spies, and did many other things to boot. Another part of her work that she had a knack for was *jailbreaks*. Captured agents or pilots were almost always shipped off to extermination camps, tortured, or executed while still in jail. If they could not escape, their days were essentially numbered. It was up to Virginia Hall and her network to free them while there was still time. Many found a second chance due to her help.

"Miss Hall displayed rare courage, perseverance and ingenuity; her efforts contributed materially to the successful operations of the Resistance Forces in support of the Allied Expeditionary Forces in the liberation of France." – President Harry Truman, Citation for Distinguished Service Cross awarded to Virginia Hall, 1945

The famous "wireless" was one of the foremost tools of the trade for a secret agent and a gadget that Virginia had to get closely acquainted with. Wireless sets were crucial tools for covert personnel during World War II, enabling them to communicate with their handlers, headquarters, and fellow agents while operating behind enemy lines. These wireless sets, radios or transceivers played a vital role in espionage, sabotage, and covert operations. These remarkable gadgets allowed agents to transmit and receive encrypted messages over long distances, maintaining secure communication channels. This was essential for coordinating activities, relaying intelligence, requesting supplies, and receiving instructions from their intelligence agencies. The specific sets used by intelligence operatives were designed to be lightweight, compact, and easily transportable. They needed to be carried inconspicuously, as agents often had to move quickly and secretly to avoid detection. The radio transmitters were often masked to resemble ordinary items. That way, they could avoid detection by the Gestapo.

Security was paramount, as intercepted messages could reveal sensitive information and compromise agents' safety. Wireless sets were equipped with encryption mechanisms to encode messages and protect them from interception by enemy forces. This was one of their most important advantages. To maintain secrecy, agents were trained to set up and operate wireless sets in hidden locations, such as safe houses, basements, or remote areas. They needed to be skilled in quickly assembling and disassembling the equipment to avoid detection. Some more advanced wireless sets employed frequency hopping, a technique that involved rapidly changing frequencies during transmission to make it difficult for enemy interceptors to track the signal. Such sets were often given to the most high-ranking agents in France. Of course, these wireless sets required a power source, which could be batteries or sometimes even hand-cranked generators. Agents had to manage their power supply carefully to ensure continuous communication while avoiding detection due to signal strength. In a famous painting of Virginia Hall, a wireless set she communicates with is shown being powered by a hand-cranked mechanism utilizing bicycle parts. It sounds odd, but it worked.

Using wireless sets posed significant risks. The transmissions could be detected by enemy direction-finding equipment, leading to the agents' location being pinpointed. To counter this, agents often used techniques like "burst transmission," which involved sending short, intermittent signals to make it harder for the enemy to locate them. agents received specialized training in wireless communication techniques, encryption, and radio operation. They needed to know how to set up the equipment, tune frequencies, send and receive messages, and troubleshoot technical issues—much had to be learned in the field on the go. One of the most famous wireless sets used during World War II was the British Paraset, a compact and lightweight radio designed by resistance operatives. Other countries, including Germany, the United States, and the Soviet Union, developed and utilized various wireless sets tailored to their specific needs. Wireless sets were essential tools that enabled agents to maintain contact with their handlers and coordinate their activities covertly and securely. These devices played a significant role in intelligence gathering, sabotage, and resistance efforts during the war.

Without them, Virginia could do little to achieve her goals during the war.

To achieve her goals as a secret agent, Virginia had to utilize any advantages at her disposal, no matter how they appeared to others. So, when forming her network, the "Heckler," she recruited all sorts of people valuable and loyal to the cause. Amongst them was Germaine Guerin, who owned a famous brothel in Lyon. Germaine helped Virginia create a network of safe houses and rescue and save Jews, allied pilots, spies, radio operators, civilians, refugees, and others in danger during the war. Moreover, owning a brothel, Guerin was a direct link to a lot of helpful information that could be heard and procured from the Germans, many of whom visited the brothel daily. According to official SOE records, it is evident that almost every British agent sent to France received some form of support from the Heckler group while it was active.

Even though she got into contact with various persons during her career in France, Virginia Hall never could relax, according to M.R.D. Foot. The official motto of every secret agent was *"Dubito, ergo sum,"* or "I doubt, therefore I survive." This means that all successful agents had to doubt anything and everyone. The successful agents who lived by this rule remained in operation without getting caught and killed. It is a well-known fact that captured agents seldom survived. Spies were sentenced to death and executed almost without exception. Virginia's lengthy tenure in France and all her successes indicate that she was a cautious and patient agent. Her "sixth sense" and caution were evident in October of 1941 when she sensed imminent danger and refused to attend a meeting of SOE agents in Marseille. This meeting was raided by the French police under German control, and dozens of intelligence operatives were captured, many meeting a sad fate. It was a significant blow to the SOE efforts in France.

After the raid, Virginia was one of the few remaining SOE agents still operating in France and the only one who could transmit information back to London. This meant Virginia was vital from then on and had to find any means to send information. She even acquired the assistance of George Whittinghill, an American diplomat in Lyon, who allowed her to smuggle reports and letters back to London in his diplomatic pouch. Virginia eventually learned that the 12 agents arrested by the French police at the SOE meeting were all incarcerated at the Mauzac prison near Bergerac. She knew she had to do something to get them out immediately; otherwise, they would all meet a terrible fate. Virginia contacted fellow agent Georges Begue, who smuggled letters from the prisoners and gave them to Virginia. Next, she recruited Gaby Bloch, the wife of one of the prisoners. Virginia recruited Bloch because she was allowed to visit her husband frequently, bringing him food, most often tins of sardines. With Gaby Bloch's help, Virginia had the proverbial "foot in the door" of the prison. Together, they devised an escape plan.

Through Gaby, Virginia smuggled in tools and materials, allowing Georges Begue to craft a key to the collective cell in which the agents were held. A wireless radio was also smuggled into the prison, and the agents were able to get in touch with London. While Gaby did her part, Virginia was getting prepared for their escape. She procured safe houses, vehicles, and various helpers. Finally, the imprisoned agents escaped on July 15, 1942, initially hiding in the woods nearby. The Germans raised an alarm and started an intense manhunt but could not successfully re-capture them. All of the imprisoned agents escaped and contacted Virginia. Afterward, they were secreted off to Spain and from there to England. Historian M.R.D. Foot called the escape "one of the war's most useful operations of its kind." Virginia's daring but successful plan allowed several agents to return to France to continue their work as operatives.

While planning for the imprisoned agents' escape, Virginia was virtually alone. She was in enemy territory, and she endured many hardships. The winter of 1941-1942 was particularly miserable, as evident from surviving correspondence with the SOE. In one letter, she complained that she could not even bathe properly. She writes, asking for soap, and says that with such a simple thing, she would be "both very happy and much cleaner." We can only imagine how difficult such a state of poverty was for a woman in a wartorn country. What is most important is that Virginia did not quit. She continued building her network of essential contacts and allies and assisted in the missions of SOE agents Peter Churchill and Benjamin Cowburn. Her expertise earned high praise from both of these men.

Once again, she displayed her foresight and caution when she avoided contact with an SOE agent, Georges Duboudin, who was sent to Lyon. She refused to introduce him to her connections and regarded him as an amateur agent who lacked security and caution. She even told the SOE headquarters to "lay off" after they required Duboudin to supervise her. In another instance, she disliked Philippe de Vomecourt, who, even though he was a French Resistance leader, lacked caution and was too grandiose in his ambitions. An interesting account of Virginia Hall survived from mid-1942 when she met with a fellow SOE agent, Richard Heslop, code-named Xavier. After their meeting, Heslop described her as a girl, even though she was 36 at the time, who lived in a gloomy apartment. Still, he depended on her to get in touch with other agents. Suspicious, Heslop asked who "Cuthbert" was. In reply, Virginia banged her prosthetic foot on the table leg, producing a hollow sound, much to their mutual amusement.

Virginia also took on the crucial task of helping British airmen, many of whom would be shot down over French skies, survive, and then find themselves in a hostile land. Once on the ground, many would find their way to Lyon - they were instructed to visit the American Consulate and say they were a "friend of Olivier." "Olivier" was another code name for Virginia Hall, who worked with the brothel owner, Guerin, and helped hide, feed, and care for numerous downed airmen. Ultimately, she would help them flee France to nearby neutral Spain and return to England.

"Those of us who had the chance of meeting her 'in action'… could never forget this very remarkable figure of the Resistance army."
- Count Arnaud de Vogue (Colonel Colomb)

Chapter IV

The Germans were angered by the daring escape of the SOE agents from Mauzac prison and the carelessness of the French police. Virginia was also in danger, as her work placed her in the spotlight. Her allies respected and admired her, while her enemies hated her. The French called her *"la dame qui boite,"* meaning "the limping lady". She found herself on their most wanted lists, being known across France. The Germans also wanted Virginia but could never find or arrest her. She was particularly sought after by the chief of the Gestapo in Lyon, the infamous Klaus Barbie, who knew of her existence as a secret agent but never knew her actual name or nationality. He reportedly said: *"I would give anything to get my hands on that limping Canadian bitch."* Due to his efforts to catch her, Barbie circulated wanted posters and placed a high bounty on her head. He knew that her secret work was disrupting his own and that the German war effort suffered because of the information she procured. Even so, he could not get his hands on her.

Virginia was a master of disguise. It was said that she could be four different women in one afternoon. It was hard to get on her trail despite her limp. The longer a secret agent stays behind the lines, the chances of their discovery and capture increase incredibly. This harsh truth was reflected in the fact that of more than 400 SOE agents sent to France, 25% did not return from their missions. Many were captured and promptly executed, while others endured brutal torture or were shipped off to concentration camps, where conditions were appalling. As we read Virginia Hall's story, we must remember that the Germans had their agents and secret police - the Gestapo - who actively tried to disrupt Allied missions and their agents' work. It was a war within a war, where spy networks created a complex battleground full of doubt and intrigue.

The German military intelligence - the Abwehr - did not sit idly while Allied agents operated. They were successful in infiltrating resistance groups and disrupting Allied sabotage networks. The German's success proved how difficult it was for Virginia Hall to remain active during the war. The Abwehr was so successful that in 1942, no active spy networks in France were operating and reporting to London. At that time, Virginia heard that a French network in Paris - one code-named Gloria - desperately needed to send reports and microfilms of German naval facilities to the Special Operations Executive in London. However, the network needed help, and Virginia rose to the call. However, she did not know that, in the meantime, the leader of the Gloria group was captured, tortured, and killed. The Abwehr itself now controlled the network. It was a perfect trap - sprung and ready to catch Virginia unaware. The Abwehr even sent its special agent, a Catholic priest who turned informant, Abbe Robert Alesh, to courier "tampered" microfilm to the drop-off point of the Heckler spy group, the office of one Dr. Rousset.

Displaying her distinct foresight and caution, Virginia did not immediately trust the Abbe, sensing the coming danger. After all, it was a dangerous time, with networks of agents collapsing all over France and the Gestapo and Abwehr working overtime. She successfully skirted around the trap and avoided capture. In September 1942, she sent an urgent message to London: *"My address has been given to Vichy… I may be watched… My time is about up."*

It was now a time of change. Virginia knew the Germans would discover and capture her if she stayed put, but escaping Lyon without being seen was not an easy task. She could not even rely on London for rescue - such an operation would be too risky and costly. Virginia was alone and knew she had to flee Nazi France and find her way into neutral Spain, where she could safely reach London. To get there - she needed the *mountains.*

Before starting her journey, Virginia stayed for another two months. During this time, she repeatedly changed her safe houses and aliases, thus avoiding capture, but the pressure was mounting. Virginia could not even complete her final mission of rescuing two jailed agents. Around early 1942, she received the news that an Allied invasion of North Africa was imminent. In response to that invasion, the Germans started their "Case Anton," a military invasion of Vichy France, which remained a largely independent zone up to that point. This operation involved the occupation of Vichy France by German forces, leading to the end of the Vichy regime's authority in the southern part of the country.

After the Allied invasion of North Africa (Operation Torch) in November 1942, the German High Command grew concerned about the possibility of the Allies advancing through French North Africa and into southern France. To counter this threat, the Germans decided to occupy the so-called "Free Zone" of Vichy France, which included the southern regions of France that were technically under French control but effectively governed by the Vichy regime, which collaborated with Nazi Germany. The German plan for the occupation of Vichy France was codenamed "Operation Lila," it consisted of two main components: Operation Anton and Operation Anton-B. The primary objective of these operations was to secure key points in southern France and neutralize any potential resistance from Vichy French forces. This was the central part of Case Anton, involving the rapid and overwhelming German occupation of the French Mediterranean coastline and the city of Toulon. The Germans feared that the French navy stationed in Toulon might fall into Allied hands or be scuttled to prevent such an occurrence. The German forces swiftly captured Toulon and other critical coastal areas. The occupation effectively ended Vichy France's control over the southern regions. The Vichy regime had collaborated with Nazi Germany. Still, this move showed that even the collaborationist government's authority was limited, and the Germans could act decisively when their interests were at stake. The Germans managed to secure the Mediterranean coastline and neutralize potential threats from the French navy. The Vichy government's influence was further reduced, and the Germans occupied strategic points that could be used to defend against possible Allied advances from North Africa. This operation consolidated German control over France and maintained its strategic position in the Mediterranean region.

Hall knew they would be hunting her, and she now had no more time. So, greatly disappointed and primarily on her own, she embarked on her flight mission, with time almost running out. Her agent and close ally, Dr. Rousset, was arrested the next day, meaning the "Heckler" group no longer existed. Virginia Hall passed through the German "forbidden zone" and traveled by train to Perpignan on November 12th, 1942. She then reached the village of Villefranche-de-Conflent by train and hired a guide for the journey ahead. From there, she began her walk into the high mountains. Virginia was so determined and undaunted, even with her artificial wooden leg. In her final contact with the SOE, she wrote that she hoped Cuthbert wouldn't trouble her. Not realizing that "Cuthbert" was the name she gave her artificial leg, SOE replied, "If Cuthbert is troublesome, eliminate him." Virginia endured the journey with Cuthbert. When she arrived at the border with Spain, she was accompanied by a guide and followed the Rotja River southward towards the mountain passes near Mantet, one of the last cities in France before the rugged Pyrenees mountains began. She went down a valley, over another pass close to Pic de la Donya, and then into Spain. Virginia made an immense effort. She walked over a 7,500-foot pass, covering up to 50 miles per day, in considerable comfort, being disabled. The terrain was rocky and rugged, and signs of civilization were few and far between.

After the high passes, they went to the Spanish towns of Setcasas and Camprodon and then to the village of Sant Juan de las Abadesas. Virginia was supposed to board a train that would take her to Barcelona. During the journey, there were many risks. This terrain was not the terrain you wanted to get lost in. Luckily, the guide knew his work well. After all, it was November. At that time, temperatures in the lower elevations of the Pyrenees can go down to the freezing point, while the mountain passes get snowed in, icy, and impassable. We can only imagine how difficult Virginia's journey had to be with her artificial leg. The constant pressure on her stump must have been unbearable at times. After two days of hard travel, Virginia reached her goals, exhausted. Alas, trouble loomed ahead. She arrived at the train station a few hours before the Barcelona train without pausing to rest. There, she was spotted by the Spanish police and jailed because she crossed the border illegally. It was such a simple fall for someone as seasoned as Virginia.

She spent a short time in jail until the U.S. Embassy intervened, and she was released. She was eager to return to France and continue her work upon release. Even though the Gestapo and Klaus Barbie's threat was too high, her wishes were refused. She wrote a letter directly to Maurice Buckmaster, the leader of the French section of the SOE. In it, she wrote:

"When I came out here, I thought I would be able to help F Section people, but I don't and can't. I am not doing a job. I am simply living pleasantly and wasting time. It isn't worthwhile and after all, my neck is my own, and if I am willing to get a crick in it because there is a war on… Well, anyhow, I put it up to you. I think I can do a job for you along with my two boys (fellow agents). They think I can too and I trust that you will let us try, because we are all three very much in earnest about this bloody war."

Maurice Buckmaster replied to Virginia in a letter in mid-1943. He writes about the dangers of Virginia's possible return to action in France:

"You are too well known in the country, and it would be wishful thinking believing that you could escape detection for more than a few days. You do realize, don't you, that what was previously a picnic, comparatively speaking, is now a real war and that the Gestapo are pulling everything they can? You will object, I know, that it is your own neck - I agree, but we all know that it is not only your own neck. It is the necks of all with whom you come into contact because the Boche (Germans) is good at patiently following trails, and sooner or later, he will unravel the whole skein if he has a chance. We do not want to give him even half a chance by sending in anyone as remarkable as yourself at the moment."

So we see the reasons why her wish was refused. Buckmaster closed the door for her return to France, and she had to make peace with that. He also went ahead and placed another proposal to Virginia. He said, *"If you are feeling that you are not pulling your weight where you are, why not come back to London and join us as a briefing officer for the boys?"* Maurice Buckmaster wanted her to come back to work with the F section of the SOE and said that her duties would be as follows:

1. *To meet them (agents) when they come back from the field, to hear what they have to say, to analyze it, and to see that their questions were answered.*
2. *To see that they are properly looked after from the point of view of material things - i.e., clothes, equipment, etc. In other words, see that the clothing and equipment officers of the F Section produce the jobs on time and correctly.*
3. *To brief the new boys with the fruits of what you have learned and what you have picked up from the latest arrivals.*

Maurice Buckmaster said that these duties sounded like the same simple "sit down" jobs she complained about and did in Spain, but he also noted that it could be an advantage. So, she worked for the SOE in Madrid for a time before returning to London in July 1943. She was quietly made an honorary Member of the Order of the British Empire (MBE). Britain's King George awarded the honor. It was essential to keep things secret because of the war and her being active as a secret agent. If the news spread and got publicized, it would uncover her whereabouts. It was a great honor for Virginia and a recognition of her extraordinary efforts. The MBE is the third-highest ranking Order of the British Empire award, behind Commander of the Order of the British Empire (COB), first and then Officer of the Order of the British Empire (OBE).

Despite her repeated requests to return to France, the SOE always declined. She was compromised, they said, and the risks were too significant. Her career as an SOE agent was over, but she was unwilling to give up so easily. She took a wireless course, getting better acquainted with the latest technologies in her service field. Then, she contacted the American Office of Strategic Services (OSS) to find work with them. The Special Operations Branch recognized her potential and hired her at the low rank and pay of a second lieutenant. One OSS agent wrote about her:

"I have interviewed the above-mentioned lady, and I feel confident that the main reason she wishes to transfer from SOE to OSS is for national reasons... She has been briefed to go in the field as a radio operator with an organizer belong to OSS, and she has again expressed a desire to go as an American body. The financial side, that is to say, the salary she might earn with OSS, has never been discussed and does not seem to worry her in any way. She merely stated that all money she might earn she would like to be sent to her mother, Mrs. E. L. Hall, Boxhorn Farm, Parkton, Maryland."

Chapter V

In her new position, Virginia Hall returned to
France on March 21, 1944, as the Allied Forces
were planning the invasion of Normandy for June
of that year. She arrived by motor gunboat at Beg-
an-Fry, east of Roscoff in Brittany. The other
option was parachuting into the location, but
with Cuthbert, that was never an option. By mid-
1944, the situation in France had drastically
changed and was about to be reversed. The Allies
were now bringing the war to its doorstep once
again. The Allied invasion of France in 1944,
codenamed "Operation Overlord," was a pivotal
military campaign during World War II that
ultimately led to the liberation of Western Europe
from Nazi occupation. The invasion began on
June 6, 1944, and is commonly referred to as D-
Day (short for "Day of Decision" or "Day of
Deliverance"). By 1944, the Allies had been
planning a major offensive against Nazi-occupied
Europe for some time. The invasion was intended
to open a new front against the Germans in

Western Europe, relieving pressure on the Eastern Front and potentially leading to the downfall of the German regime. It was a bold idea but could prove to be costly.

Extensive planning and coordination occurred in the months leading up to the invasion. General Dwight D. Eisenhower, Supreme Commander of the Allied Expeditionary Force, oversaw the operation. The Allies created elaborate deception plans to mislead the Germans about the actual location and timing of the invasion. On June 6, 1944, Allied forces launched a massive amphibious assault along the coast of Normandy, France. The attack involved American, British, Canadian, and other Allied forces. The landings occurred on five designated beaches: Utah, Omaha, Gold, Juno, and Sword. In addition to the beach landings, airborne operations were carried out the night before D-Day. Thousands of paratroopers and glider-borne troops were dropped behind enemy lines to secure critical objectives, disrupt German defenses, and pave the way for the seaborne invasion.

The beach landings were met with varying degrees of resistance. The most challenging was Omaha Beach, where strong German defenses caused heavy casualties among the American forces. However, through determination and support, the Allies managed to establish beachheads. After the initial landings, Allied troops worked to secure their positions and break out from the beachheads. They pushed inland over the following weeks and months, liberating towns and cities from German occupation. The Battle of Normandy was marked by intense fighting, including the encirclement and capture of German forces in the Falaise Pocket.

The success of the Normandy invasion enabled the Allies to establish a foothold in Western Europe. They continued their advance, liberating France and eventually pushing into Germany. This campaign marked a turning point in the war and placed significant pressure on the German forces from both the Eastern and Western Fronts. The Allied invasion of France in 1944 was a monumental undertaking that required careful planning, coordination, and immense bravery from soldiers and commanders alike. The successful establishment of a Western Front significantly hastened the downfall of Nazi Germany and paved the way for the liberation of Europe.

In that whirlwind of war, Virginia Hall again did her duty - and the job she knew best. As the Germans began their slow retreat, Virginia returned to the Haute Loire region, organizing several thousand Maquis fighters. The Maquis were rural guerrilla bands that operated in the occupied territories of several European countries during World War II. They played a crucial role in resistance movements against Nazi Germany and its collaborators, fighting for liberation, sabotage, intelligence gathering, and other activities to undermine the occupation forces. The term "Maquis" originates from the French word for the dense underbrush in mountainous regions where many of these groups were based. As members of these groups were called, the Maquisards operated primarily in the hilly and mountainous areas, using the terrain to their advantage and making it difficult for the occupying forces to locate and eliminate them. Maquis groups were often composed of local volunteers, ranging from former soldiers and partisans to ordinary citizens who opposed the occupation. They came from various backgrounds, and their motivations for joining the resistance were diverse. Maquisards engaged in various activities, including ambushes, sabotage of infrastructure (such as railways and communication lines), intelligence gathering, and supporting downed Allied pilots and other resistance members. They aimed to disrupt the occupation forces and assist the Allies by providing valuable information. The Maquis played a significant role in preparing the ground for the liberation of occupied territories.

As the Allies advanced, Maquis groups
intensified their efforts to hinder German forces,
secure vital areas, and support the Allied advance.
The Maquis received support from the Allies,
particularly regarding weapons, equipment, and
training. Allied SOE agents worked closely with
resistance groups, providing them with assistance
and guidance. With Virginia's help, their
missions could be fulfilled in earnest. Together
with her experience and skills, these groups
conducted many sabotage operations, including
blowing up bridges and destroying railways.
They all worked towards ending the German
occupation of France as fast as possible.

On her new mission in France, Virginia was
provided by the OSS with a new false identity.
She was now bearing an identification card with
the name of Marcelle Montagne, her code name -
Diane. Her main objective was to work with the
Maquis groups, helping to arm and train them
and instruct them in conducting sabotage

operations. The end goal of all this was the behind-the-lines support of the Allied invasion that would take place on June 6th, 1944. In the months before the attack, the Allied air force dropped some 10,000 tons of supplies and weapons for the Maquis behind the lines. The hard work and the risk paid off: just six months before the June 1944 invasion, the Maquis resistance, with Virginia's help, was responsible for the sabotage of more than 100 factories and the destruction of more than 1,000 locomotives in occupied France. Effectively, this halted German industry, hindering their ability to mount a solid defense.

On her new mission for the OSS, Virginia adopted a deceiving appearance. She was disguised as an older woman, wearing a gray wig and having her teeth filed down to look more like a French peasant woman. It was all about minor details that would help an agent blend in and become inconspicuous. During World War II, agents often employed various techniques to change their appearance to blend in easily, evade detection, and gather intelligence effectively. Changing one's appearance was a critical aspect of espionage, as it helped agents avoid suspicion and carry out their missions covertly. They often used disguises such as wigs, fake mustaches, beards, and glasses to alter their facial features. These disguises could help them look different from their usual appearance and make it harder for enemy agents or informants to identify them.

Agents often changed their clothing to match the local styles and attire of the region they were operating in. Wearing clothing commonly worn by locals allowed agents to blend in more effectively and avoid standing out. Changing hair color and style was a common method. Agents might dye their hair or adopt an everyday hairstyle among the locals. Changing hair color could help them avoid being recognized by individuals familiar with their natural hair color. Agents, both male and female, used makeup to alter their appearance. Makeup could help change facial features, such as making eyes appear smaller or larger or creating the illusion of scars or blemishes. Adding or removing accessories like hats, scarves, and gloves could significantly alter an agent's appearance. These items could conceal certain features or draw attention away from others. Agents often worked on adopting the local accent and manner of speech to avoid standing out as foreigners. A convincing accent could help them navigate social situations more smoothly.

They paid careful attention to local customs, behaviors, and gestures. Mimicking these mannerisms could help agents appear as part of the local community and reduce suspicion. Changing one's appearance was just one element of a more extensive set of skills and strategies employed by agents during World War II. Proper training, meticulous planning, and the ability to adapt to unexpected situations were also crucial for agents to carry out their missions successfully while avoiding detection. However, Virginia's limp always posed the risk of revealing her true identity despite the appearance changes and masks. She also thought of that and changed her gait to resemble the walk of an older woman. That way, the Germans - who knew her as the "Limping Lady" - would not suspect anything.

In France, she worked closely with Henri Lassot, the organizer and leader of the new secret "Saint" network. Virginia operated the wireless for him. Lassot, a 62-year-old seasoned agent, carried with him one million francs (roughly 5,000 British pounds at the time), while Virginia had 500,000 francs with her. These substantial amounts of money were needed to fund their missions, but Lassot wasn't up to par with Virginia. She said he was a security risk, being too talkative and careless. She understood that he could drag her down, so she quickly separated herself from him. She also instructed all her contacts to keep her whereabouts a secret from Lassot.

As she established herself in France, before

working with the Maquis, Virginia "roamed" around France in the region south of Paris. She posed as an elderly milkmaid and - true to her false identity - even made cheese. She would then sell this cheese locally to a group of German soldiers at one point. One thing that troubled Virginia while she was working in France was her American accent. Even though she spoke French, she could not speak it as a native would - such a thing required many years of practice. To avoid suspicion, she hired a French woman, Madame Rabut, who would accompany her and generally "do the talking." Behind the scenes, Virginia worked hard to establish new safe houses, organize suitable drop zones, and contact resistance groups. In Cher and Cosne, Virginia supplied several of these resistance groups with weapons and ammo, allowing them to continue their fight against the occupiers. The resistance groups had several successes. Their small-scale attacks on infrastructure and German soldiers were an effective way of disrupting the enemy. Unfortunately, not all missions were successful, however. Virginia attempted to organize a jailbreak to free three captive men in Paris. She described these captives as her "nephews," but more than likely, they were fellow agents. The operation did not succeed, as the risk of being discovered was too high.

Virginia also continued to work with the Maquis, essential for supporting the Allied Invasion of Southern France on August 15th, 1944, known as "Operation Dragoon." Operation Dragoon was a major military campaign by the Western Allies. It occurred shortly after the successful Normandy landings (D-Day) in June of the same year. The primary objective of Operation Dragoon was to establish a second front in Europe and provide support for the ongoing liberation of France from Nazi occupation. After the successful landings in Normandy (Operation Overlord), the Allied forces, led by General Dwight D. Eisenhower, aimed to capitalize on their momentum and further weaken German troops in Europe. Operation Dragoon was planned to complement the liberation efforts in northern France by creating a southern front in the Mediterranean region. The main objectives of Operation Dragoon were to liberate south France from German occupation, establish a direct supply route to support the Allied forces in northern France, and divert German resources away from the main fronts in Western Europe.

Chapter VI

The planning for Operation Dragoon began in

early 1944. It involved coordinating the efforts of the American Seventh Army, commanded by General Alexander Patch, and the French First Army, led by General Jean de Lattre de Tassigny. The invasion began on August 15, 1944, with a combined amphibious and airborne assault on the French Riviera. The landings took place along the southern coast of France, in the region between Toulon and Cannes. The American Seventh Army landed on the beaches of Provence, while the French First Army landed further to the east. The landings faced relatively light resistance compared to the heavily fortified Normandy beaches. The Allies swiftly secured the landing zones and began pushing inland. The Seventh Army and the French First Army rapidly advanced northward, encountering German defenses but making steady progress. The liberation of key cities and ports along the Mediterranean coast, including Toulon and Marseille, allowed the Allies to establish supply lines and secure important logistical bases. Operation Dragoon was successful in achieving its objectives. It liberated a significant portion of southern France, provided a crucial supply route for the Allies, and forced the Germans to divert resources from other fronts to respond to the threat.

Of course, without the efforts of Virginia Hall and her Maquis groups, it wouldn't have been so easy and successful. However, it was not always a straightforward process. Virginia did not hold rank and was a woman sent to govern primarily male soldiers. Unfortunately, women were not viewed as equal to men in those times. Virginia received orders to go to the Haute Loire department and arrived on July 14, 1944. She dropped her disguise and established headquarters in a barn near Le Chambon-sur-Lignon. However, the OSS only gave her the rank of second lieutenant, and she often had problems asserting authority over the guerilla Maquis groups, which had self-proclaimed "colonels" in charge. Due to this, Virginia complained to the OSS headquarters, telling them: *"you send people out ostensibly to work with me and for me, but you do not give me the necessary authority.*" To try and remedy it, Virginia told the Maquis and their leaders that she would finance their effort and give them arms, too - on the condition that they followed her advice and authority. Even so, the Maquis leaders caused problems. In late July, the Allies dropped three planeloads of supplies and weapons for them. Only when Virginia distributed these supplies and the money did the Maquis behave.

Together with Virginia Hall, the Maquisards in her area numbered three battalions or roughly 1,500 soldiers. They undertook several successful sabotage operations. On a larger scale, these groups were part of the French Forces of the Interior (FFI), the official designation for the French Resistance.

With Virginia's leadership, the Maquisards successfully forced the German troops to withdraw from Le Puy-en-Velay after heavy

fighting, forcing them north to retreat with the rest of the German army. Only after this and other successes did the OSS send three agents, a group called "Jeremy," by parachute, to train and supply the Maquisard battalions. Virginia, who had already done so and freed the city, was rightfully angered at this. She said: *This was after the Germans had been liquidated in the department of the Haute Loire and Le Puy liberated."*
By September 22nd, Virginia and several British and American military officers who worked for her left the Haute Loire region. They went to Paris, which by then was liberated by the Allies.

From there, together with a fellow OSS agent, Paul Golliot, she traveled to Austria to foment anti-Nazi resistance to aid in the final downfall of National Socialist Germany. Austria, annexed by Germany and fiercely loyal to the National Socialist regime, had only a few considerable resistance groups. This resistance consisted of various groups and individuals who opposed Nazi Germany's occupation and sought to resist the regime's control, maintain Austrian identity, and work towards liberation. The Austrian resistance faced significant challenges due to the country's annexation by Nazi Germany in 1938 and the subsequent repressive measures imposed by the regime. As the war ended, the voice of the liberty-loving people rose higher. Virginia came in the critical moment, helping to stir the people and move them towards action.

Some Austrians, both before and during the war, engaged in political resistance. The Austrians included individuals who opposed the Anschluss (the annexation of Austria by Nazi Germany) and maintained a sense of Austrian national identity. Some former politicians and government officials who the Nazis had marginalized continued to work against the regime secretly. Also, some various underground organizations and networks opposed the Nazi occupation. These groups engaged in activities such as distributing anti-Nazi literature, gathering intelligence, and assisting Jews and other persecuted individuals.

One such organization was the Austrian Liberation Front, which included members from different political backgrounds united in opposition to the Nazis. Writers, artists, and intellectuals played a role in resistance by creating subversive literature, art, and cultural works that challenged Nazi ideology and propaganda. Some individuals used their creative work as silent resistance against the occupiers. After all, resistance can come in many forms.

Some resistance members engaged in sabotage and small-scale attacks against German military installations, infrastructure, and supply lines. These actions aimed to disrupt the Nazi war effort and created difficulties for the occupiers. Some Austrians worked as spies or informants for foreign intelligence services, providing valuable information about Nazi activities and military plans. This contributed to the broader Allied war effort. Despite these efforts, the Austrian resistance faced challenges such as widespread surveillance, repression, and the risk of betrayal by collaborators. Nazi authorities were particularly aggressive in suppressing any signs of resistance in Austria due to its symbolic significance as Hitler's birthplace.

The Austrian resistance did not achieve the same visibility or impact as resistance movements in other occupied countries. Still, its members made significant sacrifices in their fight against the Nazi regime. Thanks to the efforts of OSS agents Hall and Golliot, anti-Nazi sentiments were rapidly spread in those final months of the war. Losing their foothold all across Europe, the National Socialists were bound to topple and fall.

The war was now drawing to a close. The Allies breached the Atlantic Wall - they entered France, spearheaded the assault, and pushed the Germans to a retreat. Now, the fighting was on *their* terrain. With enemies coming in from all sides, victory was virtually impossible. By mid-1945, Nazi Germany faced simultaneous offensives from the Western Allies and the Soviet Union on the Eastern Front. The Soviet Red Army, under the command of Marshal Georgy Zhukov, launched a massive assault on Berlin in April 1945. The battle for Berlin was fierce, resulting in heavy casualties on both sides. As the Soviet forces closed in on the city, Adolf Hitler committed suicide on April 30, 1945, in his underground bunker. With the fall of Berlin and the loss of their leader, German resistance began to collapse. On May 7, 1945, Germany signed an unconditional surrender document in Reims, France, effectively ending the war in Europe. The surrender took effect on May 8, 1945, which is celebrated as Victory in Europe or V-E Day. Celebrations erupted across Allied nations as news of the surrender spread.

Japan continued to fight in the Pacific Theater despite facing heavy bombing raids and naval blockades by the United States and its allies. The island-hopping campaign conducted by the Allies gradually brought them closer to the Japanese home islands. To avoid a prolonged and costly invasion of Japan, which was expected to result in high casualties on both sides, the United States dropped atomic bombs on the cities of Hiroshima and Nagasaki on August 6 and 9, 1945, respectively. These devastating attacks led to unparalleled destruction and loss of life, prompting Emperor Hirohito to intervene and call for Japan's surrender. On August 15, 1945, Emperor Hirohito announced Japan's unconditional surrender in a radio address, effectively ending World War II. This day is known as Victory over Japan or V-J Day. The formal surrender ceremony took place aboard the USS Missouri in Tokyo Bay on September 2, 1945, officially bringing World War II to a close.

Virginia Hall's contributions to the war effort were recognized. In September 1945, General William Donovan, the legendary head of the OSS, presented her with the Distinguished Service Cross medal. President Truman wanted to give Hall the award himself in a public ceremony, but she declined such a public event. She refused the President's awarding ritual because she was worried the fanfare would make her non-operational in the future and reveal too much to the enemy. After all, this was still the end of the Second World War, and no one was sure what a new day would bring. So Virginia chose caution once again.

Although Virginia downplayed receiving this award, the honor was immense. It was the only Distinguished Service Cross awarded to a woman during World War II and was one of the highest recognition a civilian could receive. The Distinguished Service Cross is the United States Army's second-highest military decoration awarded to someone who displays extraordinary heroism in combat with an armed enemy force. Actions that merit the DSC must be of such a high degree that they are above those required for all other U.S. combat decorations. Here is Virginia Hall's Distinguished Service Cross citation:

DISTINGUISHED SERVICE CROSS CITATION:

"The President of the United States of America, authorized by Act of Congress, July 9, 1918, takes pleasure in presenting the Distinguished Service Cross to Miss Virginia Hall, a United States Civilian, for extraordinary heroism in connection with military operations against an armed enemy while serving as an American Civilian Intelligence Officer in the employ of the Special Operations Branch, Office of Strategic Services, who entered voluntarily and served in enemy-occupied France from March to September 1944. Despite the fact that she was well known to the Gestapo because of previous activities, Miss Hall established and maintained radio communications with London headquarters, supplying valuable operational and intelligence information. With the help of a Jedburgh team, she organized, armed, and trained three battalions of French resistance forces in the Department of the Haute Loire. Working in a region infested with enemy troops and continually at the risk of capture, torture, and death, she directed the resistance forces with extraordinary success in acts of sabotage and guerrilla warfare against enemy troops, installations, and communications. Miss Hall

displayed rare courage, perseverance, and ingenuity. Her efforts contributed materially to the successful operations of the resistance forces in support of the Allied Expeditionary Forces in the liberation of France."

Sometime after the war, Virginia revisited Lyon, where she spent most of her war days. She wanted to learn the fate of those who had worked for her there. She discovered that her closest wartime associates, the brothel owner Germaine Guerin and the gynecologist Jean Rousset, were captured by the Germans and sent to concentration camps. Luckily, both survived the ordeal. Through her efforts, Virginia arranged a compensation of 80,000 francs (400 British pounds) from the United Kingdom for Germaine Guerin but could not do the same for her other friends and associates. Moreover, many of her wartime colleagues did not survive the war. She discovered that the three men she could not free from jail, her so-called "nephews," were all killed at Buchenwald concentration camp. Robert

Alesch, the Catholic priest who became a German agent and betrayed her network in Lyon, was also captured after the war and executed in Paris.

Chapter VII

The end of World War II marked the beginning of a new era of rebuilding, recovery, and global geopolitical realignment. The war's immense human and material costs underscored the importance of preventing such devastating conflicts in the future. The establishment of the United Nations in 1945 aimed to promote international cooperation, peace, and security to prevent further global disputes. In 1947, the American Central Intelligence Agency (CIA) was formed after the Second World War. Naturally, work was found for an experienced veteran secret agent like Virginia Hall. However, she was soon relegated to office and analytic work, where she remained employed for the rest of her career. There wasn't any work cut out for agents anymore. Virginia was one of the very first women hired by the CIA and was discriminated against because of her gender. The CIA later admitted this. She was deliberately passed over for promotions, honors, and work for which she was qualified. She even had the direct support of her superiors, who knew who she was and what she did during the war. Instead of building a significant career, she was essentially stuck in a desk-bound office job as an intelligence analyst. Her tasks included gathering information about the Soviet penetration of European countries.

In the 1950s, Virginia was chosen - based on her incredible wartime experience - to be the head of an ultra-secret paramilitary operation in France, which would serve as a model for establishing resistance groups in European countries in case of a Soviet attack. For many, she became a sacred presence and the first female operations officer in the entire covert action arm of the CIA. Virginia was also a valued and respected member of the Special Activities Division, supporting undercover activities to prevent the spread of communism in Europe.

Virginia's tenure as the head of the secret paramilitary operation in France occurred during a time of significant tension between the West and the Soviet Union. This time became known as the "Cold War." Much was at stake, and uncertainty reigned—this period of intense geopolitical rivalry and ideological confrontation lasted roughly from the end of World War II in 1945 until the dissolution of the Soviet Union in 1991. The term "cold" refers to the fact that the conflict never escalated into a direct military action between the two major superpowers involved: the United States and its allies on one side and the Soviet Union and its allies on the other. Instead, the Cold War was characterized by worldwide political, economic, military, and ideological confrontations.

Profound ideological differences between the United States and the Soviet Union drove the Cold War. The U.S. championed democracy, capitalism, and individual freedoms, while the Soviet Union promoted communism, state control of the economy, and collective ownership.

Both superpowers engaged in an arms race, developing and stockpiling large quantities of nuclear weapons. This race created a constant state of mutual nuclear deterrence, as each side understood that a direct military conflict could lead to catastrophic consequences. The U.S. led NATO (North Atlantic Treaty Organization), a military alliance of Western democracies. In contrast, the Soviet Union led the Warsaw Pact, a collective defense treaty among communist states in Eastern Europe. These alliances increased tensions in Europe and around the world.

The Cold War occurred through proxy wars in various regions, including Korea, Vietnam, and Afghanistan. The superpowers supported opposing sides in these conflicts, using them as arenas to compete for influence and control without directly confronting each other. The United States and the Soviet Union competed to achieve significant milestones in space exploration. The launch of the Soviet satellite Sputnik in 1957 marked the beginning of the

Space Race, which culminated with the U.S. Apollo 11 mission landing astronauts on the moon in 1969. The U.S. and the Soviet Union vied for economic dominance and sought to showcase the superiority of their respective financial systems. The Soviet Union's centrally planned economy and the United States' capitalist system competed for global influence. Both sides sought to influence global culture, media, and education to advance their ideologies and gain supporters. This included radio broadcasts, propaganda campaigns, and cultural exchanges. At various points, efforts were made to ease tensions. The period known as "détente" in the 1970s saw attempts to reduce hostility, including arms control agreements and cultural exchanges. The Cold War began to thaw significantly in the late 1980s with the reforms initiated by Soviet leader Mikhail Gorbachev. The fall of the Berlin Wall in 1989 symbolized the collapse of communism in Eastern Europe. The dissolution of the Soviet Union in 1991 marked the end of the Cold War era.

Virginia Hall was recruited as the foremost person in the secret operations in France as a part of "Operation Gladio." "Operation Gladio" was a covert network of anti-communist "stay-behind" paramilitary organizations in several European countries during the Cold War, particularly from the late 1940s to the early 1990s. The operation was initially established as a secret defense strategy to resist potential Soviet invasions or influence in Western Europe. It involved intelligence agencies and military organizations, primarily from NATO member countries. The entire operation was born out of concerns about the potential spread of communism in Western Europe after World War II. NATO and the CIA set it up as a contingency plan to create underground resistance networks in the event of a Soviet invasion or occupation. Each participating country established its own "stay-behind" network, consisting of paramilitary groups and agents who would operate covertly behind enemy lines in the event of an invasion.

These networks were to conduct acts of sabotage, gather intelligence, and organize resistance against occupying forces.

While the initial purpose of the stay-behind networks was defensive, over time, some of these networks reportedly engaged in covert and controversial activities, including espionage, propaganda, and even involvement in domestic political affairs. Allegations suggest that elements within these networks were involved in acts of terrorism and violence to shape political outcomes in their respective countries. In some instances, Operation Gladio networks have been linked to acts of terrorism, including the infamous "Strategy of Tension." This strategy involved carrying out false flag attacks and bombings to create fear, chaos, and public support for repressive measures or anti-communist policies. Some suspect that these activities aimed to discredit left-wing movements or influence elections. Operation Gladio remained largely secret until the 1990s, when investigative journalists and government officials began uncovering its existence. The revelations led to public inquiries and investigations in several countries, including Italy, Belgium, and Switzerland. These investigations aimed to shed light on the extent of the networks' activities and their possible role in domestic affairs. Many European countries eventually acknowledged the existence of their respective "stay-behind" networks.

In some cases, governments apologized for the excessive secrecy and lack of democratic oversight. Operation Gladio remains a controversial and debated aspect of Cold War history. Critics argue that the operation undermined democratic processes and led to acts of violence and manipulation. Supporters maintain that the networks served a legitimate defense purpose and that rogue elements carried out their controversial activities without official sanction. Even though Virginia Hall was essential to the Operation Gladio personnel, she was still discriminated against. In the CIA's secret report of her career, it was admitted that her fellow officers *"felt she had been sidelined - shunted into backwater accounts because she had so much experience that she overshadowed her male colleagues, who felt threatened by her"* and that *"her experience and abilities were never properly utilized."*

"She has devoted herself whole-heartedly to our work without regard to the dangerous position in which her activities would place her if they were realized by the Vichy authorities. She has been indefatigable in her constant support and assistance for our agents, combining a high degree of organizing ability with a clear-sighted appreciation of our needs… Her services for us cannot be too highly praised."
-SOE Citation for Virginia Hall

Other nations recognized her wartime efforts as well. Besides the British and the Americans, the French also decided to honor her. Their government awarded her posthumously with the

Croix de Guerre avec Palme in 1988. This was a part of their inaugural class of the Military Intelligence Corps Hall of Fame. The Croix de Guerre (Cross of War) is a French military decoration created on September 26, 1939, honoring all those who fought with the Allies against the Axis forces at any point during the Second World War.

Virginia was also honored in 2006, by the French and British ambassadors, some 24 years after her death. The honor was a ceremony at the French ambassador's home in Washington. A letter from the French President, Jacques Chirac, was read at the event, in which Virginia was characterized as a *"true hero of the French Resistance,"* paying tribute to her *"indomitable bravery, her exceptional selflessness"* and calling her a *"leader and organizer who contributed greatly to the Liberation of France."* Unveiled at the event was a unique painting of Virginia Hall, painted with oil on canvas by the artist Jeffrey W. Bass and donated by Richard J. Guggenhime. The painting depicts Virginia in a barn in wartime France, operating a wireless set as she requests supplies and personnel. It is named *"Les Marguerites Fleuriront ce Soir (The Daisies Will Bloom at Night)"*. The painting's citation was read as follows:

"When France fell under the Nazi boot in June 1940, Great Britain stood alone against the enemy. Fearing a similar fate for his country, Winston Churchill created the Special Operations Executive (SOE), an organization specializing in irregular warfare against German forces in occupied countries. SOE's early recruits for espionage operations were from a variety of people from all classes, pre-war occupations, and countries—including a 35-year-old American woman by the name of Virginia Hall from Baltimore, Maryland. Hall had seen the Nazi devastation in France firsthand and was eager to do her part to defeat fascism. She underwent SOE's rigorous preparation, remarkably, not because she was a woman, but because her left leg was made of wood, the result of a below-the-knee amputation necessitated by a pre-war hunting accident."

The British ambassador to the United States presented a certificate, signed by King George VI, to the niece of Virginia Hall. This document was supposed to be given to Hall in 1943 when she was made a member of the Order of the British Empire. However, it remained in the British government vault for over 50 years.

In 1966, it was finally time for Virginia's illustrious career to come to a well-deserved end. She turned 60 that year, the mandatory retirement age by CIA's standards. She retired from the agency where she spent her post-war years and was heavily discriminated against. Of course, her retirement did come as a welcomed change. Virginia, an older person by then, had plenty of medical problems that needed attention. So, she decided to retire and spent her retirement days living in her home in Barnesville, Maryland, with her husband, Paul Golliot.

If this name sounds familiar, it's rightly so. In 1957, Virginia Hall married Paul Golliot after the two had lived together, on and off for several years. Paul was one of her wartime colleagues. She met this dashing OSS lieutenant while stationed in Haute Loire in the war. Luck had it that both survived the war and could cultivate their love after everything had passed.

"Highly effective undercover agent during World War II, declared by Gestapo the most dangerous Allied spy. Grew up at a box horn farm nearby. Hunting accident forced partial amputation of leg, barring her from a career in the U.S. foreign service. She played a significant role in the Allied victory in France while serving in extended covert activities. In 1945, she received the Distinguished Service Cross for extraordinary heroism in connection with military operations against the enemy." ~ Maryland Historical Trust

In her retirement years, Virginia lived a quiet and simple life, deciding to live far from fame and the ever-watchful gaze of the public. She refused to sit down for an interview and chose to speak little about her life during and before the war, even to her closest relatives. Moreover, Virginia decided not to write down her memoirs, leaving those memories locked up deep inside her. Instead, she enjoyed gardening and tending to her pet poodles. As an industrious and hard-working woman, Virginia enjoyed creating things with her hands. She wove clothes for herself on a handloom and made cheese on the property. She liked solving crossword puzzles and reading history books, spy novels, and travel books from her humble library in her spare time. It was a peaceful retirement after an exciting and turbulent life full of adventure. Alas, all things come to an end eventually. Her health gradually declined, and she died peacefully at her home on July 8, 1982, at 76 years old. She was buried in the Druid Ridge Cemetery in Pikesville, Maryland, in the family plot alongside the rest of her family members. Her husband Paul died five years later on April 2, 1987, and was laid to rest beside her.

At the time of her death, the local *Baltimore Sun* did not tell of her cause of death. However, her funeral was mentioned: *"With simple services that contrasted to the drama of her World War II career, a Baltimore school girl who became the French underground's 'limping lady' was buried at Druid Ridge Cemetery in Pikesville, Maryland."* Virginia's obituary was also published in the *New York Times*, another posthumous honor. Following her death, she became a "rediscovered" icon, especially after falling into obscurity during her lifetime, as she avoided any publicity. So, in the years following her death, she inspired many, especially women and those with disabilities. She also inspired everyone interested in espionage, agents, and stories of heroism during the Second World War.

In 1988, she was again honored posthumously when her name was added to the Military Intelligence Corps Hall of Fame. Moreover, in 2016, a CIA field agent training facility was

named the "Virginia Hall Expeditionary Center."
She was inducted into the Maryland Women's
Hall of Fame in 2019.

Chapter VIII

Spies and agents, of which Virginia was one of the most famous, were many during the Second World War. Like the soldiers on the ground and the pilots in the sky, they played a crucial role in deciding the fate of the war - and the fortunes of all those involved. Their work was - almost always - located far from the battlegrounds and front lines, deep in enemy territory and conducted clandestinely. Even though it was far from the clamor and chaos of battle, the work of spies and agents was no less dangerous or essential. Being a successful spy or secret agent - or a double or triple agent - was extremely difficult. It required immense composure, bravery, and the ability to remain calm and confident when playing a role amid the enemy's forces. Today, reading the lines of this book, we can only imagine how difficult such a thing was and how terrible the constant fear had to be.

As our story of Virginia Hall takes us to the most exciting moments of espionage and covert operations in the Second World War, it is worth mentioning her other colleagues, those other heroes who contributed to the war as equally as she did. It is also worth mentioning spies who worked for the enemy as well. German, Italian, and Japanese spies employed by the Axis forces also had a role to play, even though they were on the wrong side of the war. Of course, the story of Virginia Hall would not be the same without her *enemies*.

Klaus Fuchs, for example, was a noted German theoretical physicist and an *atomic* spy who gave away some of the most precious secrets of the Allied forces. Fuchs played a significant role in passing classified information about the development of the atomic bomb to Soviet intelligence during and after World War II. During the Cold War, his espionage activities significantly impacted the global balance of power and the nuclear arms race. He was politically active from an early age and was sympathetic to left-wing and communist ideologies. He joined various left-wing organizations in Germany before fleeing to the United Kingdom in 1933 due to his opposition to the Nazi regime. During World War II, Fuchs worked on the British and American atomic bombs as part of the Manhattan Project. He held various positions, including research at the Los Alamos Laboratory in the United States, where the atomic bomb was being developed. While working on the Manhattan Project, Fuchs passed classified information about nuclear weapons development to Soviet intelligence. His espionage activities began in the late 1940s and continued until his arrest in 1950. Fuchs shared details about the design and development of the atomic bomb, as well as information about its tests. Fuchs's espionage significantly impacted the Soviet Union's ability to develop its nuclear weapons. His knowledge helped the USSR accelerate its nuclear program and build its first atomic bomb in 1949, years ahead of Western expectations. We can only imagine how difficult and stressful it had to be a spy involved in such a top-secret project - and still "get away with it."

However, other female agents who pioneered the movement in France together with Virginia Hall are also worth mentioning. Moreover, we should mention those female heroes who did not make it through their journey and paid the ultimate price while behind the lines. One such heroine was Noor Inayat Khan, a female secret agent better known as Nora Baker, or her code name - Madeleine. She was the first female wireless operator to be sent from the United Kingdom into occupied France. Khan was a remarkable British agent of Indian descent who served in the SOE during World War II. She is known for her bravery, dedication, and sacrifice as a wireless operator in Nazi-occupied France. Her story - together with the story of Virginia Hall - highlights the significant role women played in intelligence and resistance operations during the war. Noor's story is strikingly similar to Virginia's.

Noor Inayat Khan was born on January 1, 1914, in Moscow, Russia, to an Indian father and an American mother. Her father, Hazrat Inayat Khan, was a Sufi musician and teacher, and her family had a background in spirituality and the arts. She grew up in various countries, including France and England. After the German occupation of France in 1940, Khan and her family fled to England. In 1942, she joined the Women's Auxiliary Air Force (WAAF) and later applied to join the SOE, a British organization that conducted covert operations and sabotage activities behind enemy lines. Khan was selected for training as a wireless operator due to her fluency in French and proficiency in wireless communication. She completed her training and was sent to France as an undercover radio operator under the code "Madeleine." So, as we see, just like Virginia, she was an outgoing and confident woman with a youth of travel and proficiency in several languages.

Khan's role as a wireless operator was crucial for maintaining communication between occupied France and London. She transmitted vital information about German activities and troop movements to the Allies. Despite the risks, Khan remained steadfast in her duties. However, in October 1943, Khan was betrayed by a Frenchwoman and arrested by the Gestapo. She endured harsh interrogations and refused to reveal information about her work or her colleagues. Her resistance to interrogation impressed her captors. Khan made two escape attempts despite her captivity but was recaptured both times. She remained imprisoned for over a year and continued to resist. On September 13, 1944, she was executed at the Dachau concentration camp, making the ultimate sacrifice for her dedication to the Allied cause. Noor Inayat Khan's bravery and contributions have been widely recognized. She was posthumously awarded the George Cross, the highest civilian award for gallantry, by the British government. In addition, France awarded her the Croix de Guerre with a silver star. Khan's legacy lives on through various commemorations, including a memorial statue at London's Gordon Square, where she lived, and her inclusion in the "Chindits and Special Operations Roll of Honour" at the National Memorial Arboretum in the UK.

Another secret agent heroine whose story never ceases to inspire is Odette Sansom, known by her code name, Lise. She was a critical SOE agent, the first woman to be awarded the George Cross in the United Kingdom, and the Legion d'Honneur by France. Odette Sansom was born on April 28, 1912, in Amiens, France. She grew up in a bilingual household with an English father and a French mother. She later moved to England and worked as a nurse and a beauty therapist. So, like most other female SOE agents, she was bilingual. In 1942, Odette was recruited by the SOE and underwent her training. She was chosen for her

French fluency and knowledge of the country. Odette was sent to occupied France under the codename "Lise." Her primary mission was to gather intelligence, establish contacts with local resistance networks, and transmit information back to the British via wireless radio. She operated in the region of Vichy, France. Unfortunately, after working successfully for a while, Odette's cover was blown, and she was arrested by the Gestapo in 1943 along with her radio operator, Peter Churchill. She endured months of harsh interrogation, physical abuse, and solitary confinement. Despite the torture, she remained steadfast and did not reveal vital information about her mission or colleagues. Odette's resistance to her captors' demands earned her respect even from the German officers interrogating her. She famously told them, "I am not a spy, but I would have been proud to be one, as I am British." Her strong spirit and refusal to yield served as an inspiration to fellow prisoners. She was tortured, her back scorched, and her toenails pulled out, but she revealed nothing.

Odette was eventually sent to Ravensbrück concentration camp, where she endured further hardships. Despite the horrors of the camp, she continued to demonstrate resilience and solidarity with her fellow prisoners. After the war, Odette was liberated from Ravensbrück by Allied forces. She returned to England and was awarded the George Cross for her courage and unwavering commitment. The George Cross is the highest civilian award for gallantry in the face of the enemy.

What sets the story of Virginia Hall apart from the stories of all these other agents, many of whom were captured, killed, or spent their war imprisoned? As we know, Virginia avoided capture with incredible skill, unlike some of her colleagues. For example, Odette Sansom made a rookie mistake, believing a German counter-intelligence agent and quickly falling into his trap. For that, she was captured and tortured. Noor Inayat Khan also fell into the hands of the Gestapo foolishly, refusing to flee even though the danger was imminent, and yet Virginia remained "in action." That is all thanks to her incredible foresight and caution skills. Virginia could always accurately judge what would happen in the future and plan her actions based on this knowledge. Where other agents in her network rushed headfirst into danger, she took a step back - and survived. One example is the meeting of the SOE agents. She sensed a threat and refused to come: the meeting was raided, and many agents were taken away. At other times, she displayed great caution and the ability to read people: she saw other agents as suspicious or too careless. She avoided them to fulfill her missions without difficulties.

At this point, we also have to reflect upon the foremost tool in the arsenal of Virginia Hall - the *wireless radio.* The wireless was the holy grail for all agents stationed in occupied France. It was their primary way of contacting their superiors in London and the direct route to provide the most important, life-changing information to the Allies.

As such, the wireless was the primary target for the Germans, especially their secret police, the Gestapo. They went to great lengths to seize one and those who operated them. Agents had to undergo special training to run these complex machines.

Wireless operators, also known as radio operators, played a critical role throughout World War II by providing essential communication links between various military units, intelligence agencies, resistance groups, and their respective headquarters. These skilled individuals operated radio equipment to transmit and receive messages, often in code, which was vital for coordinating military operations, relaying intelligence, and maintaining contact in remote or hostile areas.

Wireless operators were a communication backbone, connecting different units and individuals across vast distances. Their ability to transmit information quickly and securely was crucial for coordinating troop movements, relaying commands, and exchanging critical intelligence. Wireless operators were stationed on ships, aircraft, and land-based units in military operations. They provided real-time communication between commanders, reconnaissance units, artillery positions, and other armed forces elements. This facilitated timely decision-making and adjustment of strategies. Furthermore, wireless operators played a pivotal role in intelligence operations. Spies and agents operating behind enemy lines relied on wireless operators to transmit information to intelligence agencies or resistance networks.

These operators were often at significant personal risk, as enemy forces could easily detect their activities. Resistance movements and special operations units like the SOE heavily relied on wireless operators. These operators, like Virginia Hall, were sent into occupied territories to establish secret communication networks, transmit information about enemy activities, organize sabotage operations, and coordinate supply drops. Wireless operators were trained to use codes, ciphers, and encryption techniques to ensure the security of their messages. These techniques were crucial to prevent interception by enemy forces and maintain operational secrecy. The work of wireless operators was dangerous and required a high level of skill and discipline. Operating radio equipment made them vulnerable to enemy detection, and if captured, operators faced the risk of interrogation, torture, or execution.

Many wireless operators demonstrated remarkable courage and determination. They often faced challenging conditions, including harsh weather, equipment malfunctions, and the constant threat of enemy patrols. Some wireless operators, like Noor Inayat Khan and Violet Szabo, gained recognition for their exceptional contributions and sacrifices. World War II witnessed significant technological advancements in radio communications, including more portable and efficient radio equipment. These advancements allowed wireless operators to transmit messages from various locations, even while on the move.

Overall, we can see that people did not have to be on the frontlines or trenches to experience war's harshness and stress. They could endure the pressure and the horror of inevitability while deep behind enemy lines, hidden out of sight while transmitting a coded message to London. They hoped the Gestapo wouldn't burst through the doors and take them away. Sometimes, the horror is in the waiting for what's about to come. Virginia Hall knew it all too well. According to many historians, the wireless operators are the true unsung heroes of the Second World War. They played a vital role in bringing about its ultimate end.

Conclusion

Once, Virginia Hall was asked why she didn't tell her fantastic story. She replied, equally simply, that she was never asked. Even so, we were able to unravel her incredible life story, preserve it for posterity, and bring to life her amazing chapter of history. As the curtain falls on Virginia Hall's remarkable journey, we find ourselves captivated by the resonance of her deeds. Her legacy transcends mere words, extending into inspiration and emulation. In the face of adversity, she exemplified the very essence of grit. In the presence of challenge, she displayed unwavering resolve. Amidst the turbulence of a world at war, she showcased the profound impact a single life dedicated to noble ideals can wield.

In her story, we can find an inexhaustible source of inspiration. We can learn of devotion to a cause, about the mind of a true warrior, about care and foresight, determination and perseverance. In the tapestry of history, Virginia Hall's thread is woven with unyielding courage, stitched with unbreakable resolve, and embroidered with the legacy of a hero who dared to shape the world around her. As we close this chapter, let us carry her torch, ignited by her unwavering commitment to justice and liberty. May her story inspire generations, lighting the way toward a world where bravery, integrity, and compassion prevail.

References:

Burges, G. 2019. *Remarkable Women: The Life and*

Times of Virginia Hall (Part 2). Rhap.so.dy In Words.

Demetrios, H. 2022. *Code Name Badass: The True Story of Virginia Hall*. Simon and Schuster.

Elder, G. 2016. *Faces of Defense Intelligence: Virginia Hall - The "Limping Lady"*. Defense Intelligence Agency.

Fausone, J. G. 2018. *Virginia Hall: An Extraordinary Woman and Exceptional Spy*. Home of Heroes.

Gralley, R. C. 2017. *A Climb to Freedom: A Personal Journey in Virginia Hall's Steps*. Studies in Intelligence Vol. 61, No. 1.

Gralley, C. 2019. *Hall of Mirrors: Virginia Hall: America's Greatest Spy of WWII*. Chrysalis Books.

Mitchell, D. 2019. *The Lady is a Spy: Virginia Hall, World War II's Most Dangerous Secret Agent*. Scholastic UK.

Mundy, L. 2019. *Female Spies and Their Secrets*. The Atlantic.

Pearson, J. 2023. *Wolves at the Door: The True Story of America's Greatest Female Spy*. Rowman & Littlefield.

Purnell, S. 2019. *A Woman of No Importance: The Untold Story of WWII's Most Dangerous Spy, Virginia Hall.* Little, Brown Book Group.